ACORN SOUP

ACORN SOUP
by L.FRANK

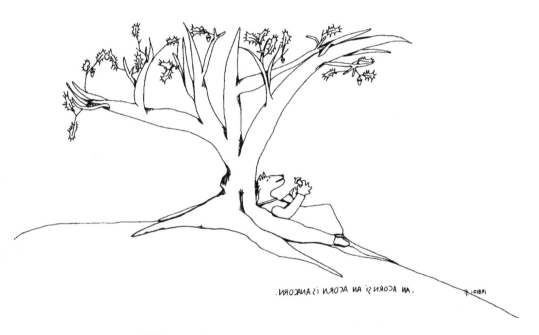

. AN ACORN IS AN ACORN IS AN ACORN.

HEYDAY BOOKS • BERKELEY, CALIFORNIA

Library of Congress Cataloging-in-Publication Data

Frank, L.
    Acorn soup / L. Frank.
        p.   cm.
    ISBN 1-890771-14-7
    1. Indians of North America--Humor.   2. Indians of North America--Caricatures and cartoons.   I. Title.
    E98.H77M35   1998
    970.004'97002'07--dc21   98-33182
                                                                                    CIP

Cover art: "Coyote Brings Home the Bacon" by L. Frank
Back cover photo by Sharon Joerger
Book Design: Jeannine Gendar

Please address orders, inquiries, and correspondence to:
    Heyday Books
    P.O. Box 9145, Berkeley, CA 94709
    Phone (510) 549-3564, fax (510) 549-1889
    heyday@heydaybooks.com

Printed in Canada
10 9 8 7 6 5 4 3 2 1

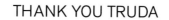
THANK YOU TRUDA

CONTENTS

INTRODUCTION

An interview with L. Frank

I grew up in southern California in the fifties, in a house full of dachs-hunds and robust, blond half-siblings. There I was, skinny and dark and fascinated by Indians. I knew I was part Indian, but I always thought I was Apache. I spent a lot of time studying Plains Indians on horses. At 28 I found my father and a whole California Indian family who are proud to be Indian—but keep in mind they were all raised in Hollywood.

When I was a child, I would have dreams about being taken up into the sky and then let go. Finally, not long after I began learning about my father's people, I took off. I was flying, I could see every-thing, I was wonderful, and nobody could get close to me, because I could fly. I heard some people laughing, and they were laughing at me, not with me. I looked around and I saw ravens, and they were saying, "She's the dumbest, slowest thing we've ever tried to teach, but once she's got it, she's really got it."

I think the more southern your tribe is in California, the harder it is to get a grip on your cultural heritage. But we've got good hunting skills—we've got fax machines and e-mail, and we can get on the freeway and hunt down people who can explain things for us. I found out my family is Tongva (sometimes called Gabrielino) and Ajachmem (or Juaneño), which I have also seen spelled 'Axatcme, Acagchemem, Ajcachme, Ajashmay, and several other ways. I had to find people to explain where all these words came from. We didn't have a written language, so how do I know they're not *all* wrong?

Trying to learn about the language, I came across the word for a rattle made of cocoons. It was winter, and I scoured the hillsides of central California in the snow, looking for these special cocoons. I didn't find any, but it got me away from the television for a while.

Finally, someone sent me some cocoons. I was so proud of my progress, I was showing the cocoons to everyone. An elderly Mewuk woman drew back from them and I didn't know if she was dismayed or repulsed or what. I learned you shouldn't show them to just any-body, but I didn't know why.

Trying to make string to hold the rattle together, I gathered Indian hemp from a field in Sonoma County, and I learned how to make string, and then we went to court to try to keep a developer from cutting down the hemp. Then I got into astronomy, and then I made some stone bowls—the first stone bowls of the Tongva people in over two hundred years—with soapstone mined from Catalina Island.

Sometimes when I'm working with soapstone, I can hear the voices of the ancestors. Once I made a bowl that was so perfect, so flawless, I knew it was the ancestors who had made it. And once I was weaving a basket, in my brother's back yard in Orange County, and over the fence I could hear a lot of women talking, joking about a man they knew. Then I realized they were not speaking English; I was hearing the voices of the people who used to live there.

Why I write backwards

One of my favorite explanations came from a woman who said she'd been trying to understand for years, and finally she decided I was working from inside the drawing—like when they used to stand behind those glass weather maps on the TV news and draw on them with grease pencils—so of course the writing was backwards.

Where the drawings come from

My eyes are getting bad and my dyslexia's getting worse, so I've given up reading for entertainment now, except for real-life family murders and horror stories. Usually, I'm totally immersed in academic papers and books. As I'm reading, I hear what people in my tribe and surrounding tribes have said. I remember something I've learned. I apply it to what I'm reading, and then I come up with tertiary things. This and this—what they said and what those other people said—add up; two colors are going to create a third color. So in that third color I have my own understandings. And that's where the drawings come from.

I don't visualize the drawings. My head is so full that when I sit down to draw, I'm not really even there. At that point, I honestly don't feel like I have anything to do with it. I warm up first; I draw little things and they're really ugly and stupid and contorted, and after that I turn to a clean page, and then next thing I know, the page is done and I'm just trying to remember what the date is. I know that I've been visiting that tertiary place. Everybody's opinions are rolling around in my head. The scientists say something about our language or our cooking or our boats, Indians have told me how they feel about it, my own understanding has been developing, and that's the creation point.

After being immersed in native cultures from across the United States for so long, when I began to learn about California cultures I was amazed and overwhelmed. I think that born-again enthusiasm comes through in the early drawings. Early on, a friend made me a fur hat, and when she handed it to me—this big raw thing—I jumped. She said, "You're afraid of fur, aren't you?" Coming from L.A., I was wondering if all the guts were scraped out. I didn't know the hat would be soft, and it would smell just delicious. The drawing of a person wearing that thing with the deer legs hanging down the back and saying "Yipes!" came out of that experience.

Some of the earliest drawings are about the death of Wiyoot. Wiyoot was the son of creation, one of the first people, and when he died it was the first time death had come into the world. Rabbit (Tuuvit) used a rattle of cocoons to sing a mourning song, and that initiated dance. So, in my beginning drawings, where he's unclothed and dancing around logs and stuff, and more physically a rabbit, that's the Indian-times rabbit. And then later on, when he's going to art galleries, he's still the rabbit, but contemporary. He's filled out a bit, because our diets have changed.

Wiyoot was created when the sister and the brother mated and made the earth. Plants and trees and rocks were made, and then Wiyoot was one of the first people. He was murdered, poisoned by Red-legged Frog (a woman scorned). The people decided to cremate him, and they needed somebody to go and get fire for the funeral pyre. Since they weren't sure how Coyote would act, what he would do with the body—what he would do anywhere—they tried to get rid of him, telling him to go get some fire and then come back. And he kept going away, but shorter and shorter distances, because he knew they were going to be doing something and he was going to be deliberately left out. So he kept running back asking, "Where is my father? I want to see him," speaking of Wiyoot. The people were standing in a ring around the pyre, and he came back again and leaped over the shortest people, saying, "Where is my father, where is he?" And then he bit the heart of Wiyoot and ran off with it. People tried to beat him with the sticks they were using to poke the fire, and that's why he's colored the way that he is, and ragged looking.

That's what the drawings that say "No greater love hath any Coyote for his father" are about. It's Coyote's nature to grab the heart or whatever else is around that he can get at the moment, and yet he's acting from some kind of profound love, all at the same time.

When Wiyoot died, a lot of people metamorphosed—some into trees, some into animals, some into rocks. When he was dying, Wiyoot said he'd be back in three days. So he came back as a new moon. The new moon was always a time of great importance, when the elders and doctors and people of importance would get together and discuss philosophical, spiritual things.

Stories of a dying god who is resurrected are unusual, and the Spanish missionaries were fascinated with the parallels to their own religion. In fact, Boscana wondered where they had learned these stories that were to him so obviously Christian, "notwithstanding their imperfect as well as fabulous description." This attitude had an unfortunate impact on the Native people who fell under the influence of the missionaries. That's where "Trust Me" and the other mission drawings came from.

One of the drawings that a lot of people respond to is the one of a woman holding a basket of acorns. I was so surprised to hear people thought it was an expression of hope and abundance. What they don't realize is that her short hair means she is mourning. She's holding tightly to what is left of her way of life. The more someone learns about California cultures, the more they'll understand.

People point out irony or double entendres or this or that in my work that I never notice. Once, someone was praising the "stark, minimalist background" in one of my paintings. What I didn't tell him was that black was the only color I had at the time.

A few of the drawings have to do with the selling of art, the selling of the culture—"I hope the wine and cheese are good," for instance. I call the selling of Indians and Indian art "Indians on Parade."

There was a show recently at the American Indian Contemporary Arts gallery in San Francisco where a lot of people came in off the streets. "This is Indian art" is all the information they got. The titles, which tell half the story, were hard to see. So people just had the drawings—blam—in front of them. I heard a woman asking her friend, "Well, do you understand what's happening here?" "No," she said, "but I know something is…" As she went around the room it was forming a picture for her and she was getting the gist of it.

I didn't know that paintings and etchings would come from draw-ings. I only started painting watercolors because I had a class and a teacher I really liked, Faith Wilding, and she did watercolors, and showed me Georgia O'Keefe. So I used to do plants, but they didn't look like Georgia O'Keefe's, of course. Then I fell in love with etching. I'm addicted to the smell of the acids and the inks. I really like the line drawings as etchings, a lot.

I've been working in soapstone again, too. The other day, a friend of mine brought over a big power tool. I was ready to rough out some dolphins—it's just the gross work, some pieces that always have to come off, and it doesn't matter who does it. I was so excited about being able to do it quickly that I sawed half the flukes right off. Didn't mean to. They're going to be caught in fishing nets, I think, Japanese tuna nets or something—it's going to be a whole diorama. No, I can't do that, I have to start afresh.

Once I start making them, all the joy comes back. And they go through so many stages, and I'm so particular with them. I think I'm ready to go a little bit further and make just the feeling of, the understanding of, the emotion of a dolphin. I'm ready to be happy with something, and I think it's going to be them.

Some drawings just happen when people make me mad, or a situation is aggravating but I don't want to be hostile and bitter because it's a waste of time. Sometimes I can feel when I'm being a smart aleck, but sometimes I just can't help myself. Native indicators, for instance. I imagine them as something you would hold close to somebody, like those old mood rings, and pieces would change color if the person was a native, had the right DNA or blood quantum or whatever.

It ties into "Coyote as a Simple Man." It doesn't do to take ourselves too seriously. I had a job in an Indian gallery—I only worked one day a week, and even that was too many in a row for me—and one day my boss came in and said, "You're doing such a great job! People come in and they rave about you, and they buy things. I'm going to give you a raise!"

"Great!" I said.

He said, "How do you do it?"

I said, "I'll show you." And I did. Usually I had my shoes off, because I'd been napping under the Navajo blankets. I'd stand in the corner with my shoes off. I wouldn't help people when they came in. Sometimes they filled out their own ticket books and made their own change. I did this stoic native in the corner, the wooden Indian. Don't drop the cigars...

The title? It's from the Marx Brothers' "Duck Soup."

I. JUST AFTER THE BEGINNING TIME

12591

LIKE A MOTH TO THE
FLAME
COYOTE TO THE
HEART.

#92991

21

COYOTE ON THE
ROAD TO WISDOM
SANS MAP.

22

NO GREATER LOVE HATH ANY COYOTE FOR HIS FATHER.

23

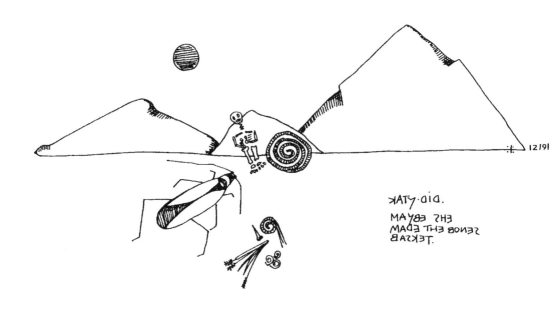

KATY·DID.

MAYBE SHE
MADE THE BONES
BASKET.

12191

24

Wyjoot HAS RETURNED.

25

II. MISSION TIMES

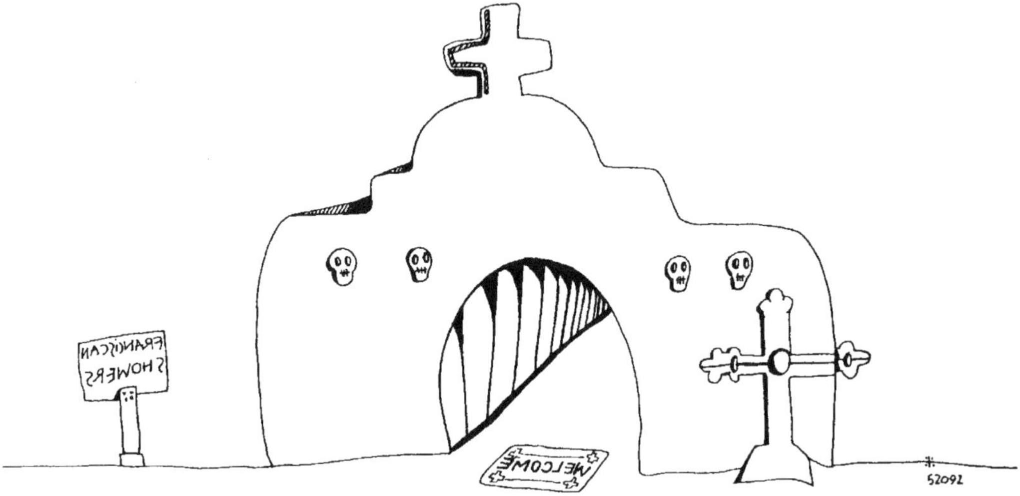
FRANCISCAN
SHOWERS
WELCOME

TRUST ME. #103191

NO REALLY PLEASE
TAKE MY WIFE...

COYOTE THEATER

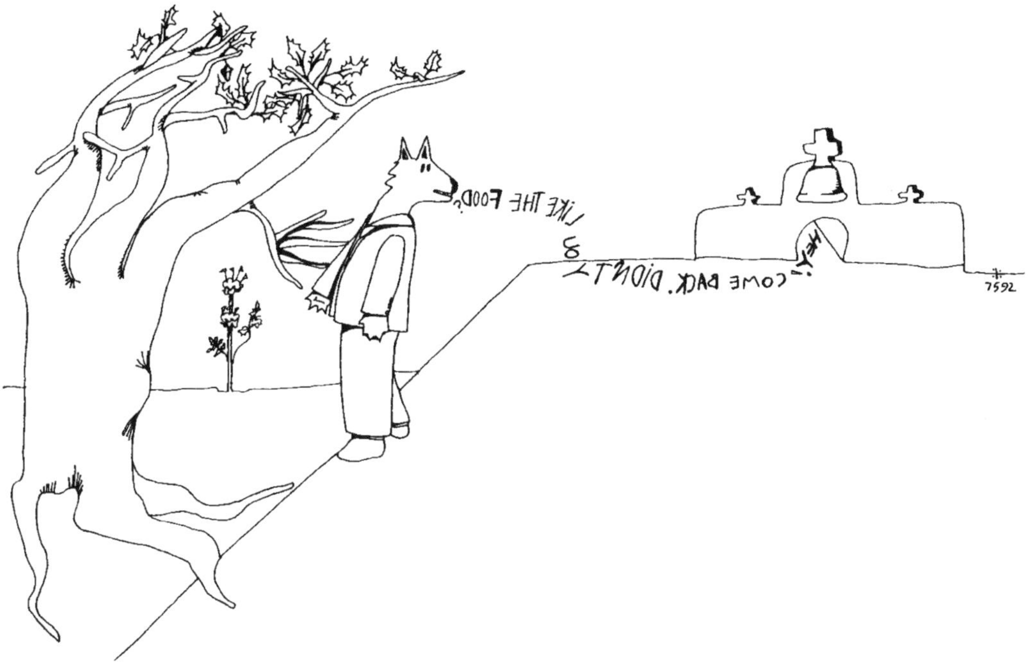
HEY! COME BACK. DIDN'T YOU LIKE THE FOOD?

STOP THE DANCE.

31

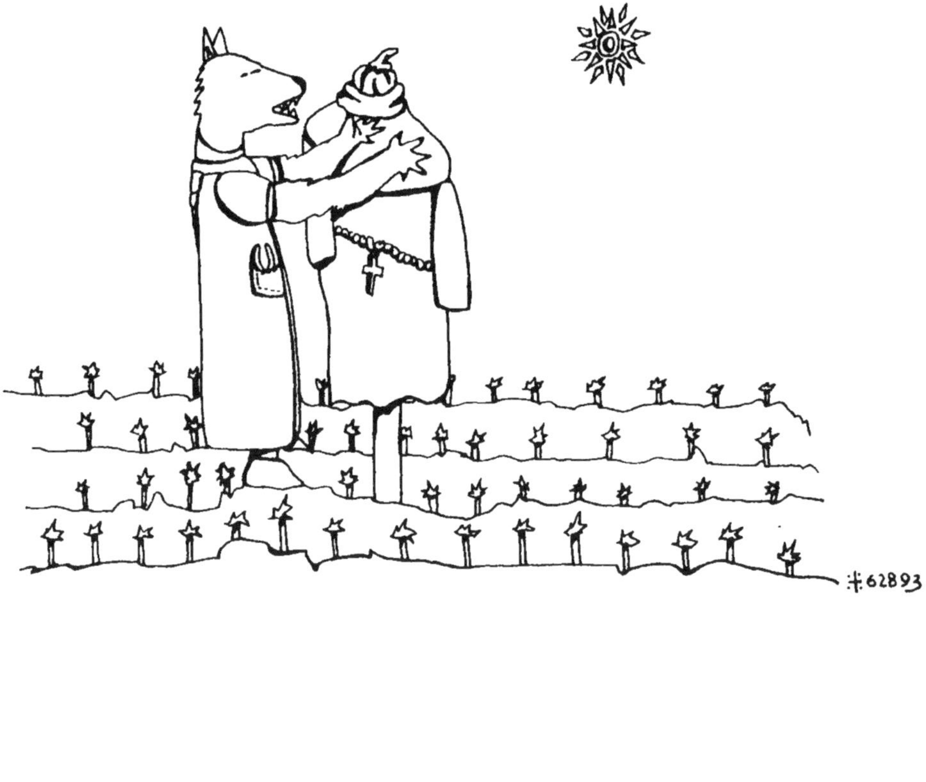

III. INDIANS ON PARADE

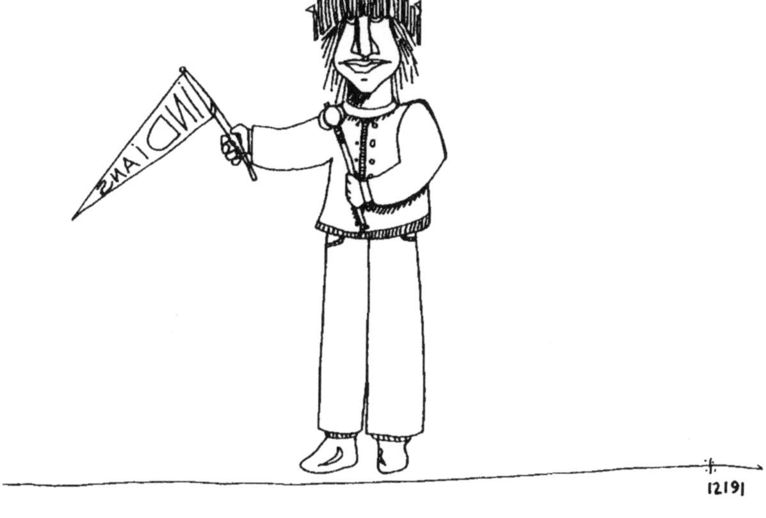
INDIANS

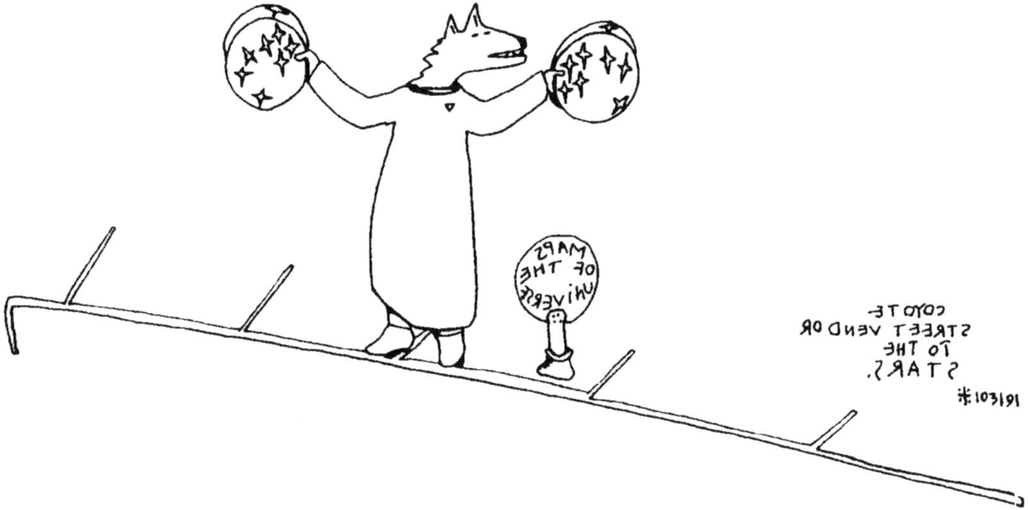
MAPS OF THE UNIVERSE
COYOTE- STREET VENDOR TO THE STARS.

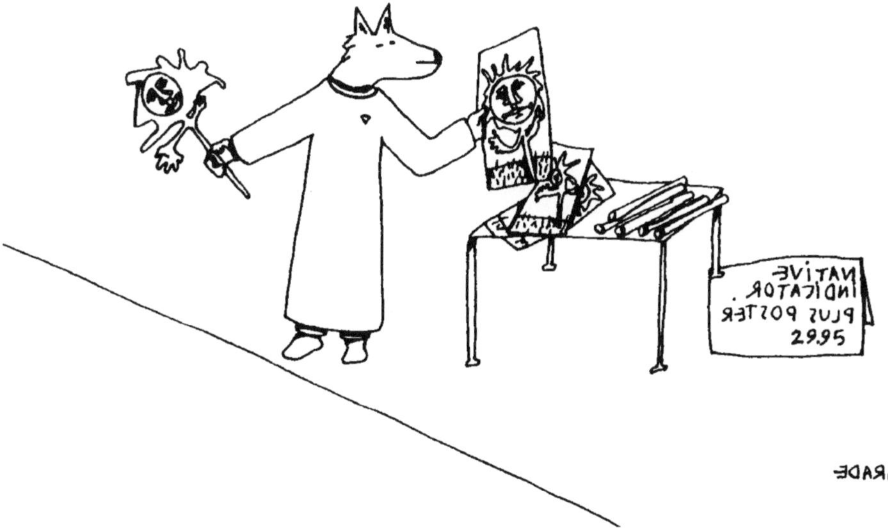
NATIVE
INDICATOR.
PLUS POSTER
29.95

101891

COYOTE CAMPS
ALONG THE PARADE
ROUTE.

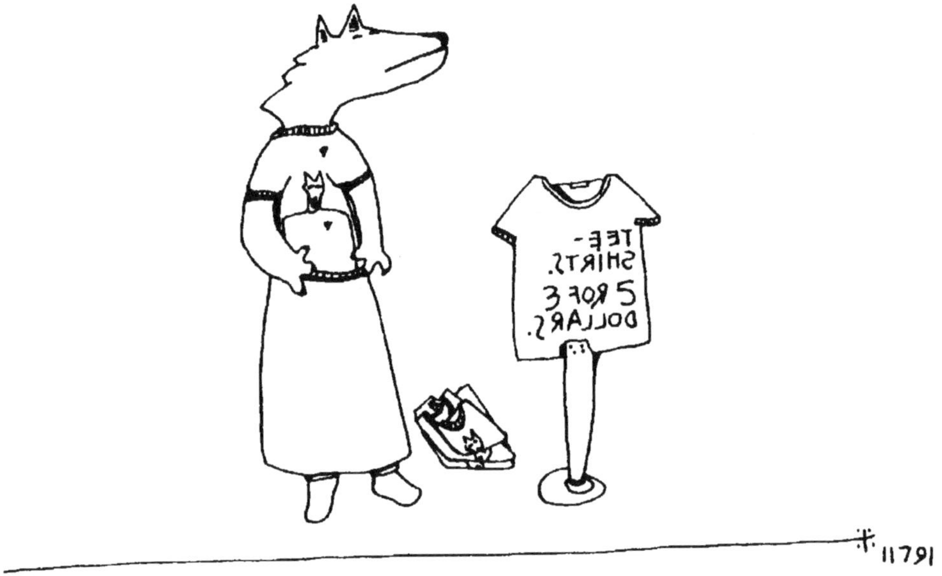
TEE-
SHIRTS.
DOLLARS.

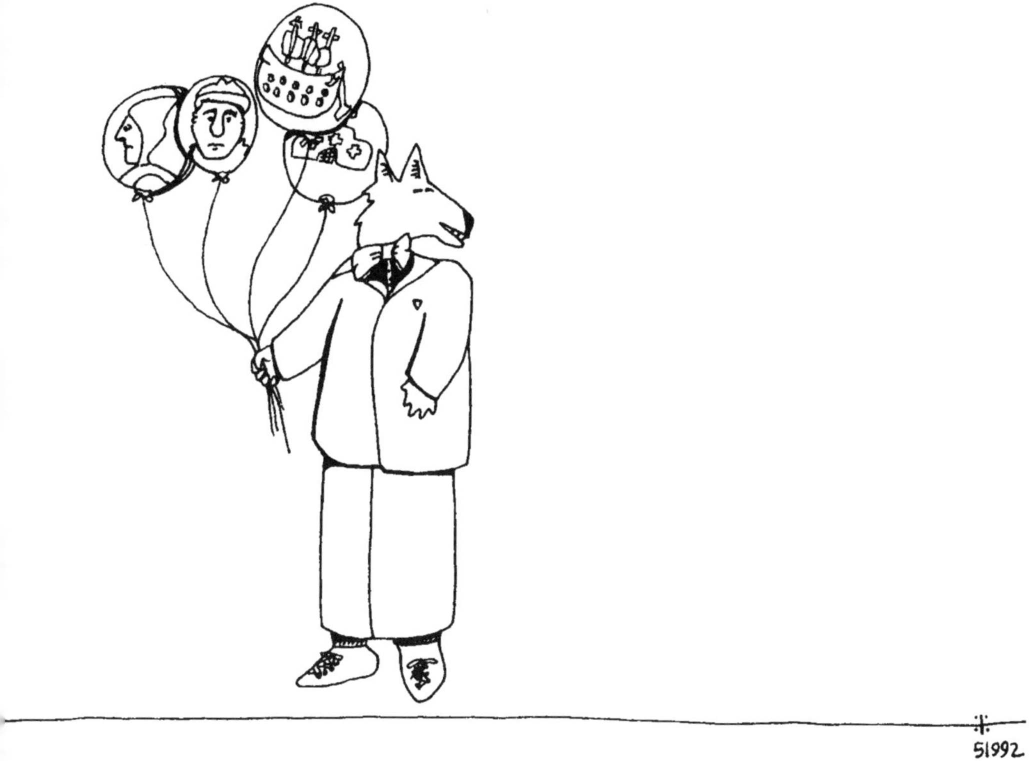
51992

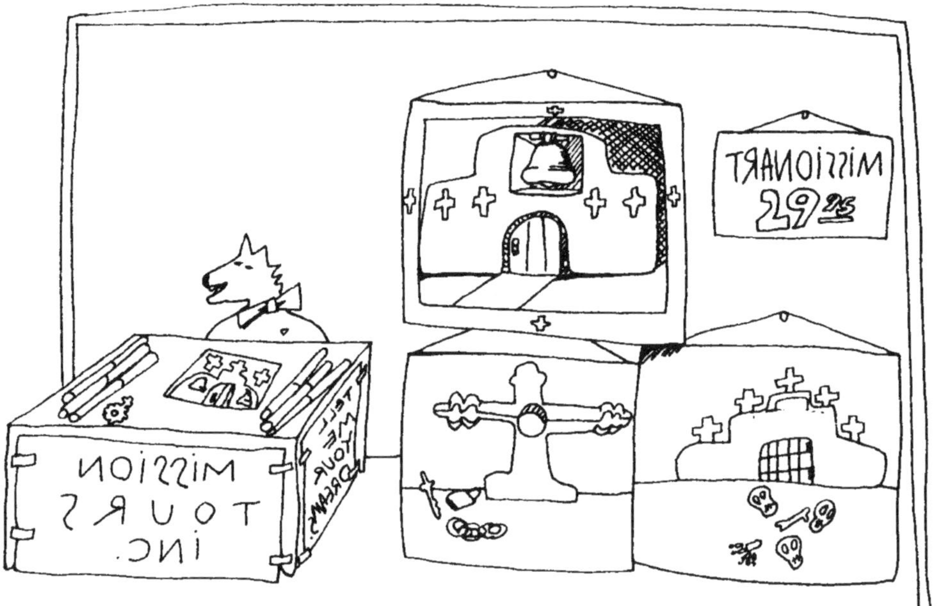
MISSIONART
MISSION TOURS INC.
TELL ME YOUR DREAMS

CALIFORNIA POW WOW.

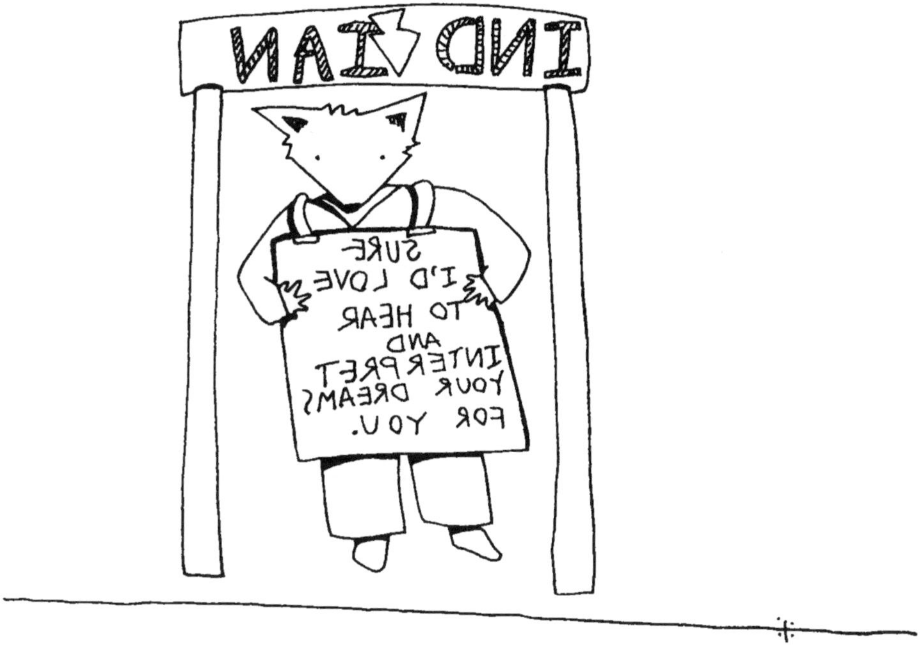
INDIAN
SURE I'D LOVE TO HEAR AND INTERPRET YOUR DREAMS FOR YOU.

IV. NOW ABOUT THEN

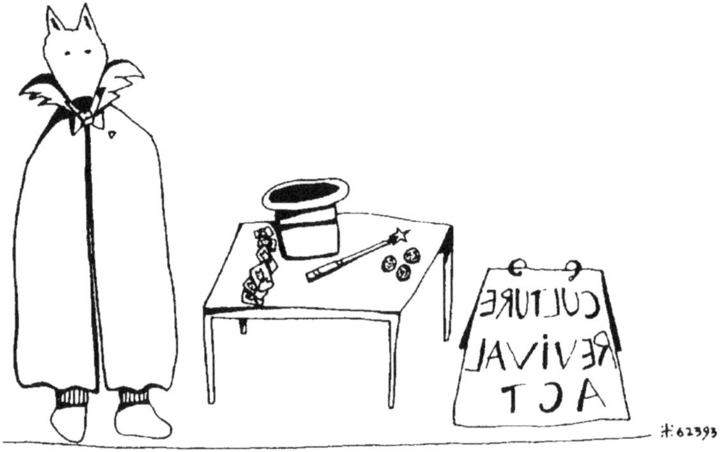
CULTURE
REVIVAL
ACT

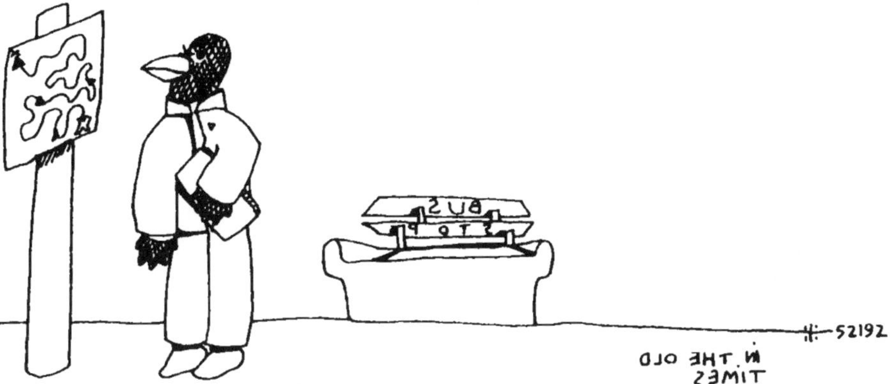
BUS
STOP

IN THE OLD
TIMES
THE CROW
WOULD SIMPLY
FLY.

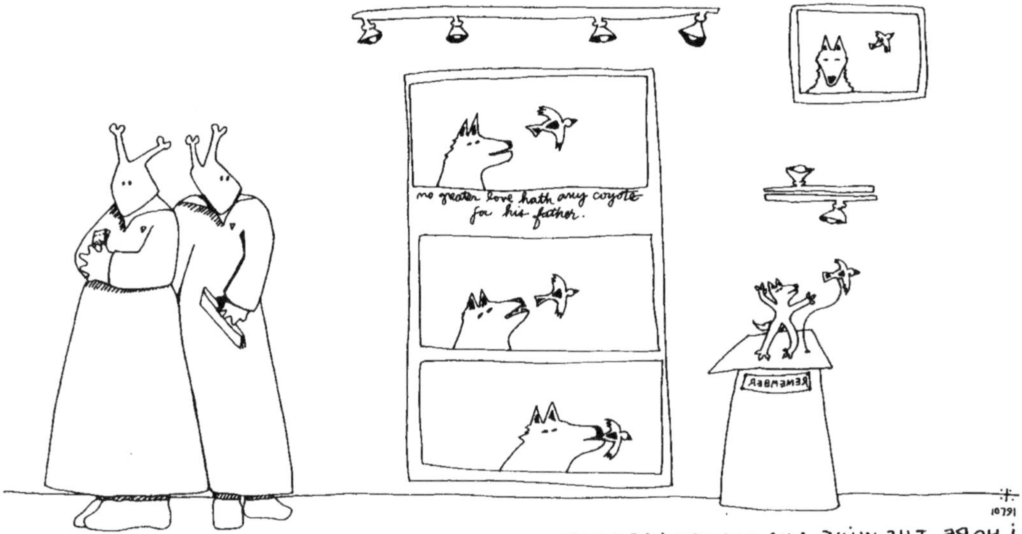
no greater love hath any coyote
for his father.
REMEMBER

i HOPE THE WINE AND CHEESE ARE GOOD...

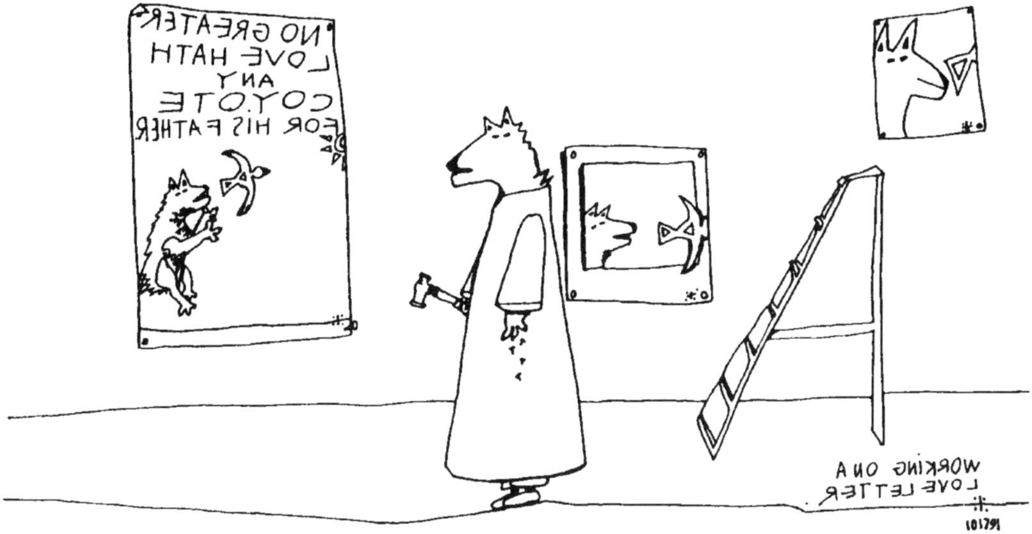
NO GREATER LOVE HATH ANY COYOTE FOR HIS FATHER
WORKING ON A LOVE LETTER

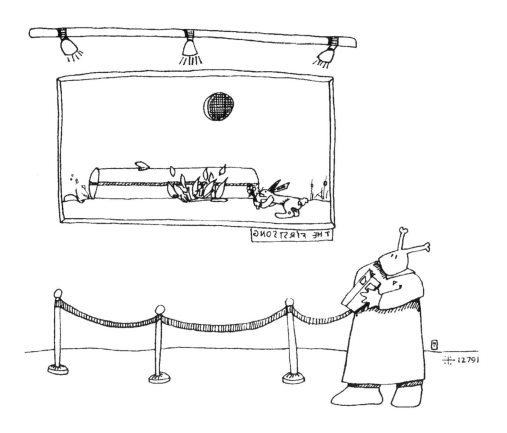

44

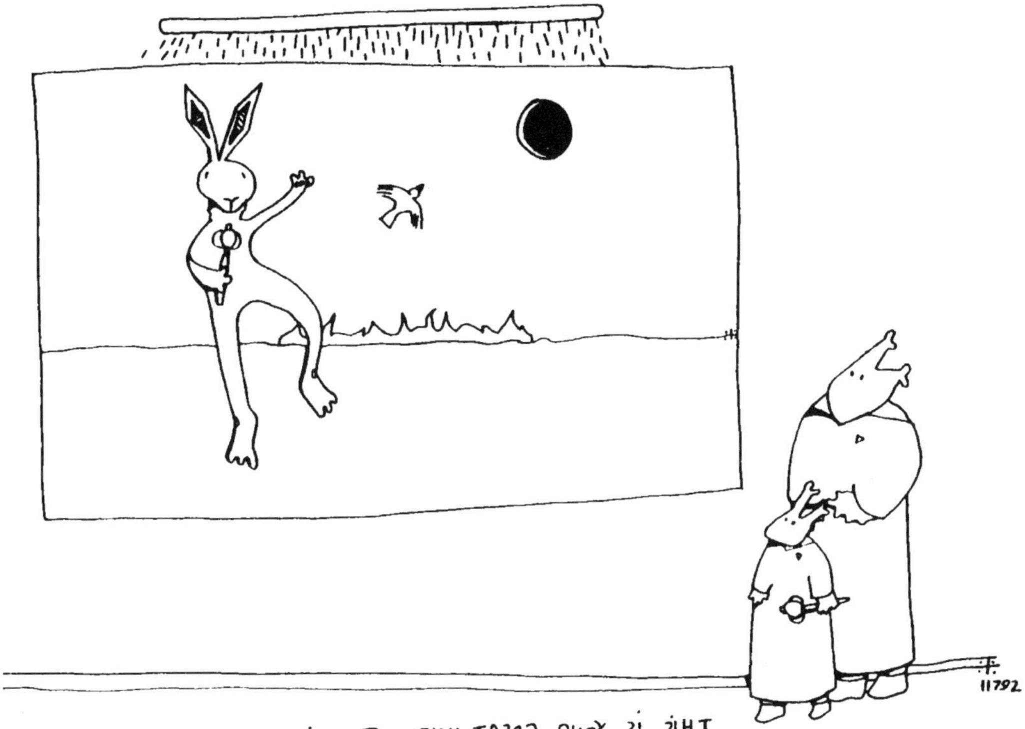

THIS IS YOUR GREAT UNCLE TOOVIT.

STARRY
NIGHT.
☀11191

46

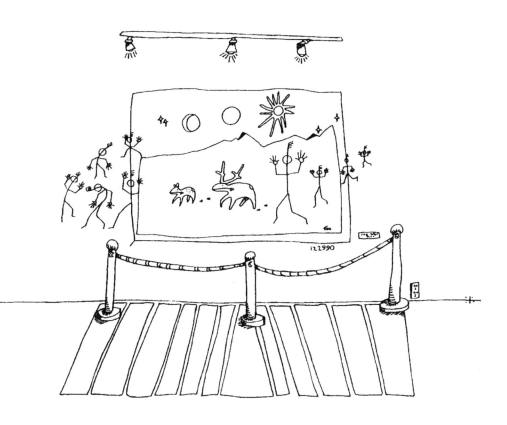

122990

COYOTE REMEMBERS AND WONDERS IF OTHERS WILL.

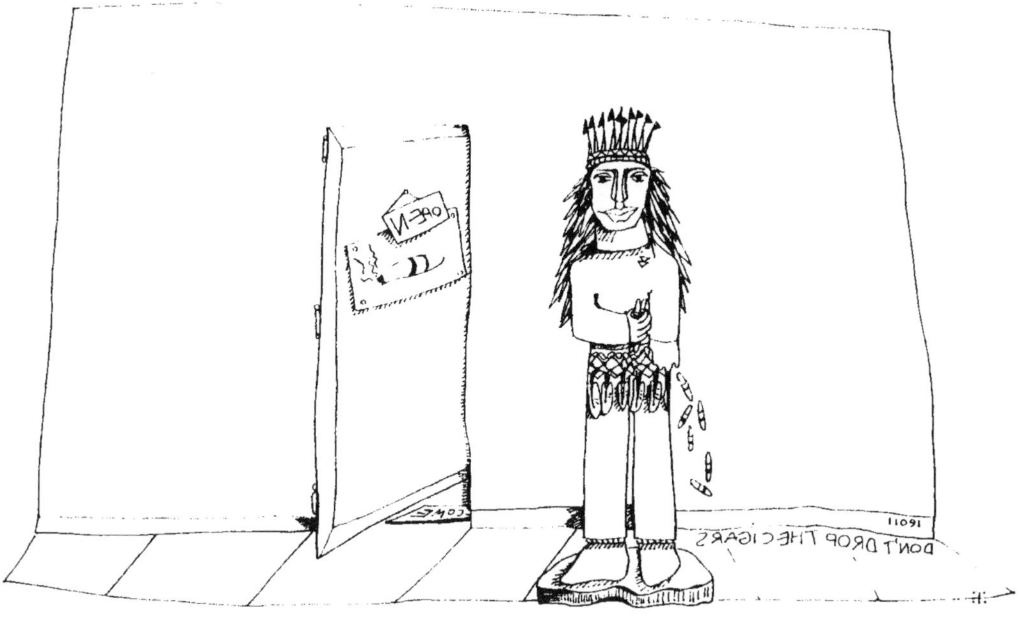
OPEN
DON'T DROP THE CIGARS

V. MORE NOW ABOUT THEN

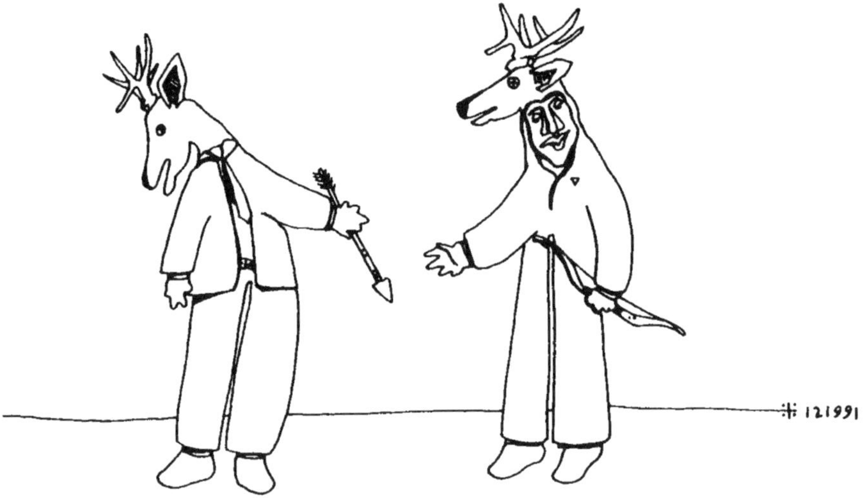
⁂ 121991

SINCE THE DEATH OF WOYOTE THE DEER GIVE THEIR BODIES TO THE HUMAN BEINGS.

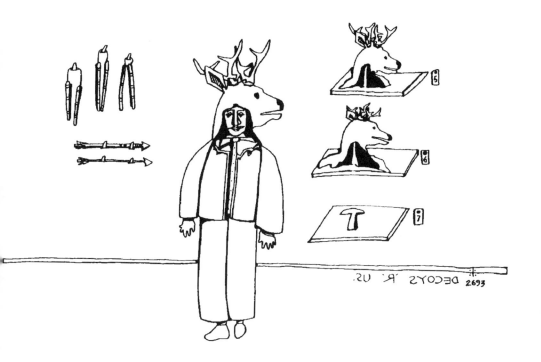

DECOYS "R" US. 2693

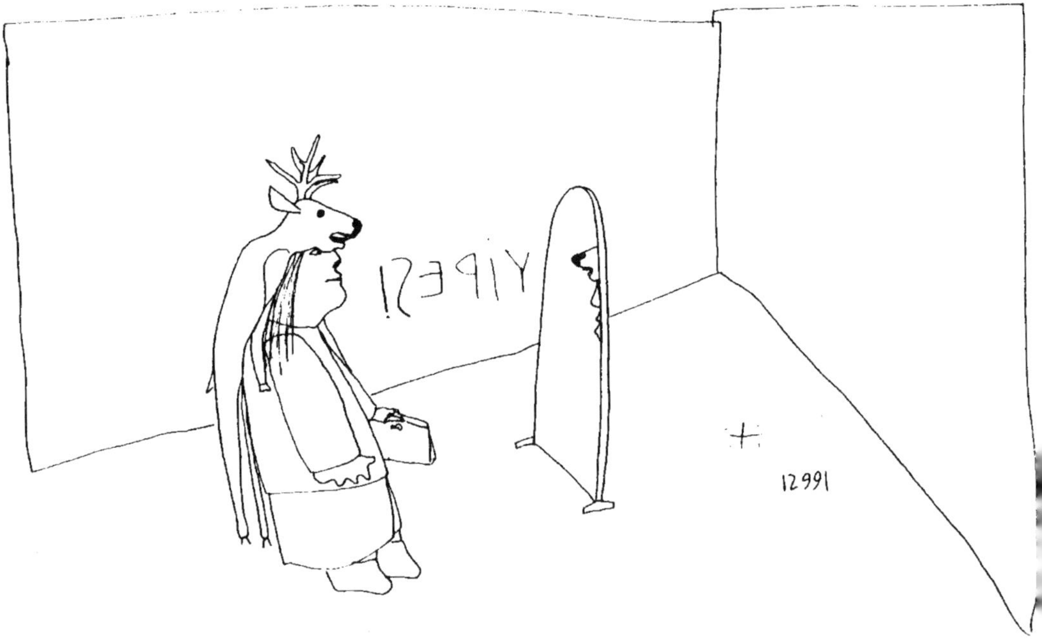
YIPES!

53

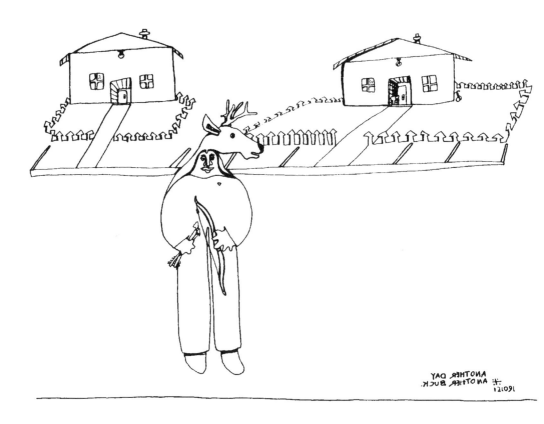

ANOTHER DAY
ANOTHER BUCK.
121091

54

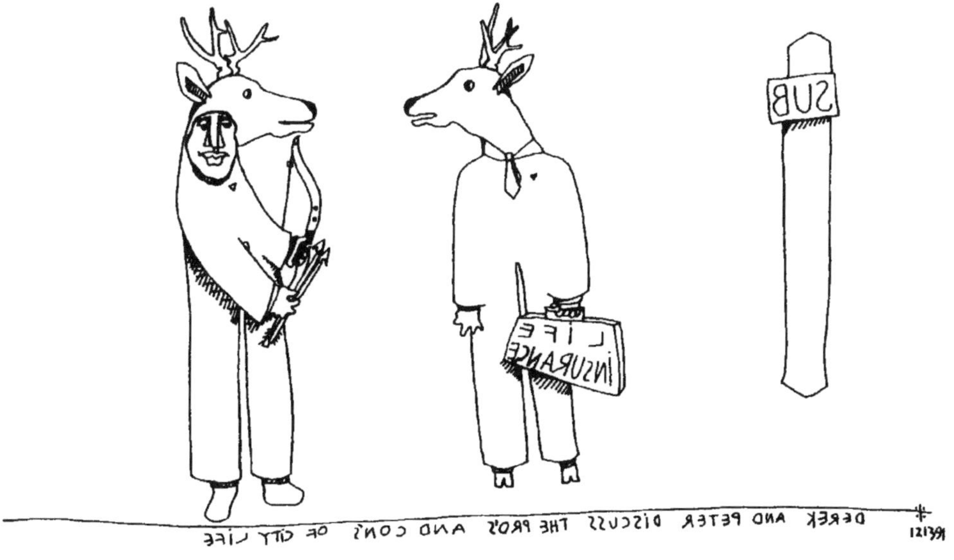
SUB
LIFE INSURANCE
DEREK AND PETER DISCUSS THE PRO'S AND CON'S OF CITY LIFE

BUS LOAD OF DEER HUNTERS.

VI. COYOTE AS A
SIMPLE MAN

亢 9996

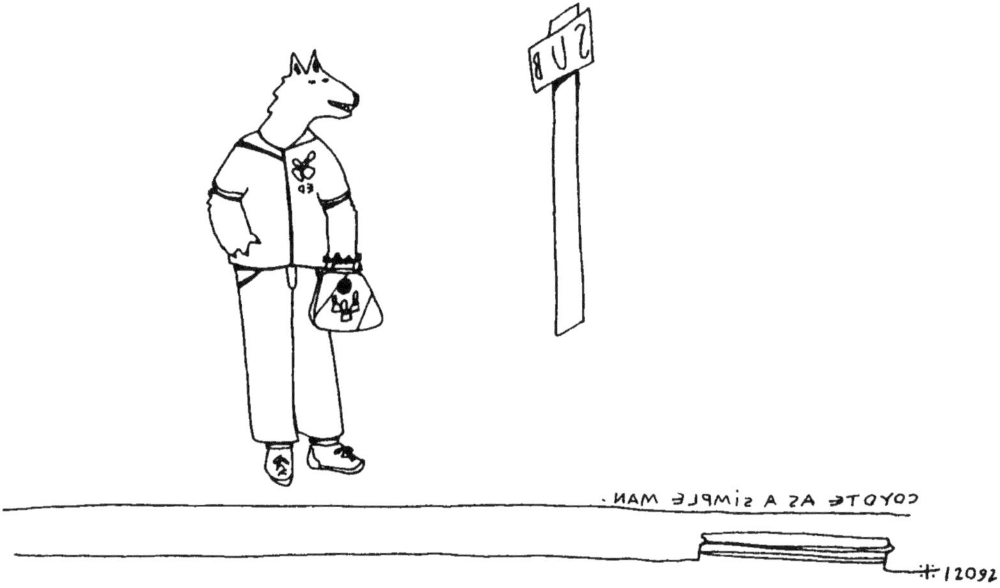
BUS
COYOTE AS A SIMPLE MAN.

SACRED
INDIAN
DOINGS

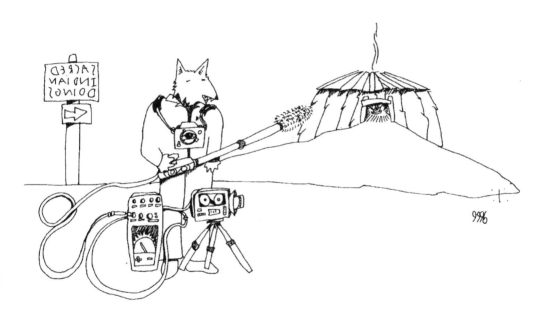

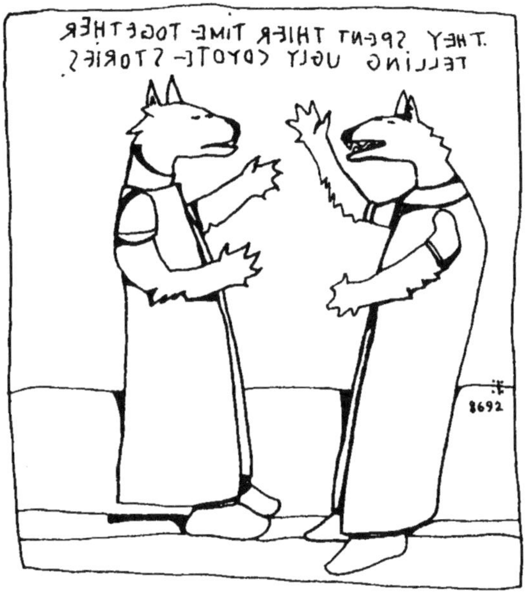
THEY SPENT THIER TIME TOGETHER
TELLING UGLY COYOTE-STORIES.

COYOTE AS A SIMPLE MAN.

✳ 11292

APPENDIX

I. Just After the Beginning Time

This is the time of the creation of earth and sky, plants and animals and finally the first people. A man called Wiyoot became a leader… some say bad, some say good. His life is ended when he scorns a woman. Wiyoot's is the first death in the world. At this time the earth ends its expansion, all living things metamorphose into their present forms, and with the introduction of death into the world all things are drastically changed.

19. The cycle of creation.
20. The first cremation: Tuuvit sings the first mourning song.
21. Coyote biting the heart of the slain Wiyoot.
22. Coyote on the road to wisdom sans map.

23. Coyote risks everything jumping into the funeral pyre to eat the heart of Wiyoot.
24. After the pyre burned down, Wiyoot's bones were gathered in a basket—the first ever made. The maker was either a red-legged frog or a katydid.
25. Some of the people who observed Wiyoot's resurrection as the new moon. Quail once had more head feathers but in the process of mourning they were singed off, leaving the topknot we see today.

II. Mission Times

Indian world order ends as the Spanish arrive with their world order and the two do not mix.

26. The outcome of culture clash.
27. The old "forked tongue" routine.
28. All unmarried women and girls were incarcerated in monjerios at the missions. Many did not survive this experience.
29. It was more than bad or insufficient food that motivated the natives to run away.
30. The years of missionization have left contemporary Indians juggling now with then.
31. A woman mourning the old even as the magic continues around her.
32. Be afraid. Be very afraid.

III. Indians on Parade

This is the place where the dominant society feels safe having us Indians around… in parades, logos for sports teams, and on the silver screen. And sometimes we natives buy into this picture of us. We camp along the parade route selling remnants of our culture.

33. Rah! Go Braves! Go Warriors! Go Chiefs! Scalp 'em! Rah!
34. Coyote is often responsible for the placement of stars in the sky.
35. Native indicators for my Cherokee friends and the B.I.A.
36. Large, X-large, XX-large…
37. Coyote on the parade route selling revisionist history.
38. Coyote offers the revisionist tour.
39. Party talk.

IV. Now About Then

We spend our time remembering Indian time while being confronted by now.

40. In order for many natives to revive their cultures they must navigate the quagmire of the many disciplines of anthropology, linguistics, astronomy, and ethno-this and ethno-that. And find dollars to support the revival. Native people are proficient magicians.
41. Nothing is as straightforward as it once was.
42. I worry that at my art shows the refreshments are more refreshing than my art and I hope the show as worth the parking structure fees.
43. Artistic homage to an ancient belief.
44. I was walking through a museum with Lucy
45. Parker looking at early, large photos of California Indians and she was related to several of the subjects.
46. The magic goes on all around us.
47. The museum dance. The magic goes on all around us.
48. The Tongva people find their sea legs.
49. I am pretty sure the quote "It's hard to be an Indian these days" was spoken by Julian Lang.

V. More Now About Then

After the introduction of death into the world everyone searched for a place free from death. They found no such place, and the deer were the first to offer themselves as food. Deer hunting was/is more than men with bows and arrows. It is a trade between people (the deer and humans): my life so yours may continue.

50. A relationship is born
51. Early on, being a true consumer, I pondered where one might purchase a hunting wardrobe.
52. Checking out the fur disguise for believability.
53. The ritual deer dance before the hunt.
54. The old nine to five.
55. Strange bedfellows.
56. This is my favorite.

VI. Coyote as a Simple Man

Coyote... a complex philosophical construct in our minds but, really, just an everyday Joe.

57. Coyote dressed for the bucolic ball.
58. Coyote Ed on his way to Tuesday night bowling.
59. Tapes and CDs available.
60. Drawing gone awry.
61. Coyote in his new natural habitat.

Cover: Coyote bringing home the bacon.